To

_____

From

To the Members of our
1st Marriage 911 Class

Wil & Cheryl Steplight
November 2006

Love Is Forever

*Lessons for Couples
from God's Holy Word*

Brighton Books
Nashville, TN 37203

The quoted ideas expressed in this book (but not scripture verses) are not, in all cases, exact quotations, as some have been edited for clarity and brevity. In all cases, the author has attempted to maintain the speaker's original intent. In some cases, quoted material for this book was obtained from secondary sources, primarily print media. While every effort was made to ensure the accuracy of these sources, the accuracy cannot be guaranteed. For additions, deletions, corrections or clarifications in future editions of this text, please write BRIGHTON BOOKS.

Scripture quotations are taken from:

The Holy Bible, King James Version

The Holy Bible, New International Version (NIV) Copyright © 1973, 1978, 1984, by International Bible Society. Used by permission of Zondervan Publishing House. All rights reserved.

The Holy Bible, New King James Version (NKJV) Copyright © 1982 by Thomas Nelson, Inc. Used by permission.

The New American Standard Bible®, (NASB) Copyright © 1960, 1962, 1963, 1968, 1971, 1972, 1973, 1975, 1977, 1995 by The Lockman Foundation. Used by permission.

Holy Bible, New Living Translation, (NLT)copyright © 1996. Used by permission of Tyndale House Publishers, Inc., Wheaton, Illinois 60189. All rights reserved.

The Message (MSG)- This edition issued by contractual arrangement with NavPress, a division of The Navigators, U.S.A. Originally published by NavPress in English as THE MESSAGE: The Bible in Contemporary Language copyright 2002-2003 by Eugene Peterson. All rights reserved.

The *International Children's Bible®, New Century Version®.* (ICB) Copyright © 1986, 1988, 1999 by Tommy Nelson™, a division of Thomas Nelson, Inc., Nashville, Tennessee 37214. Used by permission.

New Century Version®. (NCV) Copyright © 1987, 1988, 1991 by Word Publishing, a division of Thomas Nelson, Inc. All rights reserved. Used by permission.

The Holman Christian Standard Bible™ (HCSB) Copyright © 1999, 2000, 2001 by Holman Bible Publishers. Used by permission.

Cover Design by Kim Russell / Wahoo Designs
Page Layout by Bart Dawson

ISBN 1-58334-218-4

Printed in the United States of America

Table of Contents

Introduction

Now these three remain: faith, hope, and love.
But the greatest of these is love.

1 Corinthians 13:13 HCSB

The familiar words of 1st Corinthians 13 remind us of the importance of love. Faith is important, of course. So, too, is hope. But love is more important still.

Christ showed His love for us on the cross, and, as Christians, we are called upon to return Christ's love by sharing it. We are commanded (not advised, not encouraged . . . commanded!) to love one another just as Christ loved us (John 13:34). That's a tall order, but as Christians, we are empowered to meet the challenge.

This text contains 30 Biblically-based principles for Christian couples. These devotional readings, when taken to heart and put into practice, can help you make love last forever.

Each devotional reading contains Scripture, thought-provoking essays, and quotations from noted Christian thinkers. If you are fortunate enough to be involved in a loving relationship, offer a prayer of thanks to God. And then, use the ideas in this book to help you make *your* great relationship even greater.

1

Love Is Forever

You are my God, and I will give you thanks;
you are my God, and I will exalt you.
Give thanks to the LORD, for he is good;
his love endures forever.

Psalm 118:28-29 NIV

God's love for you is deeper and more profound than you can fathom. And now, precisely because you are a wondrous creation treasured by God, a question presents itself: What will you do in response to God's love? Will you ignore it or embrace it? Will you return it or neglect it? The decision, of course, is yours and yours alone.

When you and your loved one embrace God *together*, you are forever changed. When you embrace God's love, you feel differently about yourself, your marriage, your family, and your world. When you embrace God's love together, you will share His message and you will obey His commandments.

When the two of you accept the Father's grace and share His love, you will be blessed here on earth *and* throughout all eternity. So, if you genuinely seek to build a marriage that will stand the test of time, make God the centerpiece. When you do, your love will endure forever.

God's love is measureless. It is more: it is boundless.
It has no bounds because it is not a thing but a facet
of the essential nature of God. His love is something
he is, and because he is infinite, that love can enfold
the whole created world in itself and have room for
ten thousand times ten thousand worlds beside.

A. W. Tozer

Life with Christ is endless love; without Him,
it is a loveless end.

Billy Graham

The great love of God is an ocean without
a bottom or a shore.

B. H. Spurgeon

The unfolding of our friendship with the Father
will be a never-ending revelation
stretching on into eternity.

Catherine Marshall

God has pursued us from farther than space
and longer than time.

John Eldredge

*For the Lord is good. His unfailing love continues forever,
and his faithfulness continues to each generation.*

Psalm 100:5 NLT

❧ A Prayer ❧

Thank You, Lord, for Your love. Your love is boundless,
infinite, and eternal. Today, let us pause and reflect upon
Your love for us, and let us share that love with all those
who cross our path. And, as an expression of our love for
You, Father, let us share the saving message of Your Son
with a world in desperate need of His peace.

Amen

❧ More Verses to Consider ❧

Psalm 32:10
Psalm 117:1-2
Psalm 100:4-5
John 15:9

2

Building on a Firm Foundation

---

*But God demonstrates His own love toward us,
in that while we were still sinners, Christ died for us.*

Romans 5:8 NKJV

I s your relationship built upon the firm foundation of God's love? Are you willing to obey God's commandments and to welcome His Son to rule your heart? Hopefully so. As you and your spouse grow in the love and knowledge of the Lord, you will also grow in your love for each other.

The 19th-century writer Hannah Whitall Smith observed, "The crucial question for each of us is this: What do you think of Jesus, and do you yet have a personal acquaintance with Him?" Indeed, the answer to that question determines the quality, the course, and the direction of our lives *and* our relationships.

The old familiar hymn begins, "What a friend we have in Jesus…." No truer words were ever penned. Jesus is the sovereign Friend and ultimate Savior of mankind. Christ showed enduring love for His believers by willingly sacrificing His own life so that we might have eternal life. Now, it is our turn to become *His* friend.

Let us love our Savior, praise Him, and share His message of salvation with our neighbors and with the world. When we do, we demonstrate that our acquaintance with the Master is not a passing fancy; it is, instead, the cornerstone and the touchstone of our lives *and* our relationships.

This hard place in which you perhaps find yourself is
the very place in which God is giving you opportunity
to look only to Him, to spend time in prayer,
and to learn long-suffering, gentleness, meekness—
in short, to learn the depths of the love that
Christ Himself has poured out on all of us.

Elisabeth Elliot

So Jesus came, stripping himself of everything as he
came—omnipotence, omniscience, omnipresence—
everything except love. "He emptied himself"
(Philippians 2:7), emptied himself of everything
except love. Love—his only protection,
his only weapon, his only method.

E. Stanley Jones

He loved us not because we're lovable,
but because He is love.

C.S. Lewis

Behold, behold the wondrous love,
That ever flows from God above
Through Christ His only Son, Who gave
His precious blood our souls to save.

Fanny Crosby

*And I am convinced that nothing can ever separate
us from his love. Whether we are high above the sky
or in the deepest ocean, nothing in all creation
will ever be able to separate us from the love of God
that is revealed in Christ Jesus our Lord.*

Romans 8:38–39 NLT

A Prayer

Dear Jesus, You are our Savior and our protector.
Give us the courage to trust You completely.
Today, we praise You, we honor You, and we will
live according to Your commandments, so that
through us, others might come to know
Your perfect love.
Amen

More Verses to Consider

*1 John 5:1
John 10:11
John 15:13
John 15:9*

3

Love Is Kind

O God, thou art my God; early will I seek thee:
my soul thirsteth for thee, my flesh longeth for thee in
a dry and thirsty land, where no water is; To see thy power
and thy glory, so as I have seen thee in the sanctuary.
Because thy lovingkindness is better than life,
my lips shall praise thee.

Psalm 63:1-3 KJV

The noted American theologian Phillips Brooks advised, "Be such a person, and live such a life, that if every person were such as you, and every life a life like yours, this earth would be God's Paradise." One tangible way to make *your* world a more godly place is to spread kindness wherever you go. And remember: kindness begins at home . . . but it should never end there.

For Christian couples, kindness is not an option, it is a commandment. Jesus teaches, "In everything, therefore, treat people the same way you want them to treat you, for this is the Law and the Prophets" (Matthew 7:12 NASB). Jesus did not say, "In some things, treat people as you wish to be treated." And He did not say, "From time to time, treat others with kindness." Christ said that we should treat others as we wish to be treated in everything. This, of course, isn't always easy, but as Christians, we are commanded to do our best.

Today, as you consider all the things that Christ has done in your life, honor Him by being a little kinder than necessary. Honor Him by slowing down long enough to say an extra word of encouragement to your loved ones. Honor Him by picking up the phone and calling your partner for no reason *other* than to say, "I'm thinking of you and I love you." Honor Christ by obeying the Golden Rule. He expects no less, and He deserves no less. And so, by the way, does your beloved.

If we have the true love of God in our hearts,
we will show it in our lives. We will not have
to go up and down the earth proclaiming it.
we will show it in everything we say or do.

D.L. Moody

Be so preoccupied with good will
that you haven't room for ill will.

E. Stanley Jones

When you extend hospitality to others,
you're not trying to impress people,
you're trying to reflect God to them.

Max Lucado

The mark of a Christian is that he will walk
the second mile and turn the other cheek.
A wise man or woman gives the extra effort,
all for the glory of the Lord Jesus Christ.

John Maxwell

Do all the good you can. By all the means you can.
In all the ways you can. In all the places you can.
At all the times you can. To all the people you can.
As long as ever you can.

John Wesley

Carry each other's burdens,
and in this way you will fulfill the law of Christ.

Galatians 6:2 NIV

❧ A Prayer ❧

Dear Lord, help us see the needs of those around us.
Today, let us spread kind words of thanksgiving
and celebration in honor of Your Son. Let forgiveness
rule our hearts, and let our love for Christ be reflected
through the acts of kindness that we extend
to each other and to those who need
the healing touch of the Master's hand.
Amen

❧ More Verses to Consider ❧

Proverbs 11:17
Proverbs 16:24
Titus 3:2
Romans 12:10–12

4

Love
Takes Time

*If we love one another, God abides in us,
and His love is perfected in us.*

1 John 4:12 NASB

L ove is always a choice. Sometimes, of course, we may "fall in love," but it takes work to stay there. Sometimes, we may be "swept off our feet," but the "sweeping" is only temporary; sooner or later, if love is to endure, we must plant our feet firmly on the ground. The decision to love another person for a lifetime is much more than the simple process of "falling in" or "being swept up." It requires "reaching out," "holding firm," and "lifting up." Love, then, becomes a decision to honor and care for the other person, come what may.

Love requires time. Period. If you sincerely wish to build your relationship and keep building it, you should invest large quantities of your time and energy in the care and nurturing of your loved one. And as you spend time together, you should do your very best to ensure that God remains squarely at the center of your family's life. When you do, God will bless you and your marriage in ways that you could have scarcely imagined.

Being a Christian means accepting the terms
of creation, accepting God as our maker and redeemer,
and growing day by day into an increasingly
glorious creature in Christ, developing joy,
experiencing love, maturing in peace.

Eugene Peterson

Real love has staying power.
Authentic love is tough love.
It refuses to look for ways to run away.
It always opts for working through.

Charles Swindoll

A Christian is never in a state of completion
but always in the process of becoming.

Martin Luther

What is Christian perfection?
Loving God with all our heart, mind,
soul, and strength.

John Wesley

I'm not what I want to be. I'm not what I'm going to be.
But, thank God, I'm not what I was!

Gloria Gaither

*Love never gives up. Love cares more for others
than for self. Love doesn't want what it doesn't have.
Love doesn't strut, Doesn't have a swelled head,
Doesn't force itself on others, Isn't always "me first,"
Doesn't fly off the handle, Doesn't keep score of the sins
of others, Doesn't revel when others grovel,
Takes pleasure in the flowering of truth, Puts up
with anything, Trusts God always, Always looks for
the best, Never looks back, But keeps going to the end.*

1 Corinthians 13:4-7 MSG

❧ A Prayer ❧

Dear Lord, You have given us the gift of love;
let us share that gift with others. And, keep us mindful
that the essence of love is not to receive it,
but to give it, today and forever.

Amen

❧ More Verses to Consider ❧

*2 Peter 3:18
1 Corinthians 13:11-13
Hebrews 6:1
Philippians 3:14*

5

The Power of Our Thoughts

*Finally, brethren, whatever things are true,
whatever things are noble, whatever things are just,
whatever things are pure, whatever things are lovely,
whatever things are of good report, if there is any virtue
and if there is anything praiseworthy—
meditate on these things.*

Philippians 4:8 NKJV

How will you direct your thoughts today? Will you obey the words of Philippians 4:8 by dwelling upon those things that are honorable, true, and worthy of praise? Or will you allow your thoughts to be hijacked by the negativity that seems to dominate our troubled world? As you are deciding how to focus your thoughts and energies, be forewarned: the quality of your relationships will tend to mirror the quality of your thoughts.

Are you fearful, angry, bored, or worried? Are you so preoccupied with the concerns of this day that you fail to thank God for the people He has brought into your life? Are you angry, worried, bitter, or pessimistic? If so, God wants to have a little talk with you.

God intends that you experience joy and abundance in every aspect of your life, including your relationships, but He will not force His joy upon you. You and your loved ones must claim God's abundance for yourself. So, today and every day thereafter, celebrate the life that God has given you by focusing your thoughts and your energies upon "whatever things are of good report." Today, count your blessings instead of your hardships. And thank the Giver of all things good for gifts that are simply too numerous to count . . . starting, of course, with your marriage.

The things we think are the things that feed our souls.
If we think on pure and lovely things,
we shall grow pure and lovely like them;
and the converse is equally true.

Hannah Whitall Smith

Preoccupy my thoughts with your praise
beginning today.

Joni Eareckson Tada

Christian love, either towards God or towards man,
is an affair of the will.

C.S. Lewis

Attitude is all-important. Let the soul take
a quiet attitude of faith and love toward God,
and from there on, the responsibility is God's.
He will make good on His commitments.

A. W. Tozer

*Those who are pure in their thinking are happy,
because they will be with God.*

Matthew 5:8 NCV

∽ A Prayer ∾

Lord, we pray for an attitude that is Christlike.
Whatever our circumstances, whether good or bad,
triumphal or tragic, let our response reflect
a God-honoring attitude of optimism,
faith, and love for You.
Amen

∽ More Verses to Consider ∾

*Colossians 3:2
Proverbs 16:3
Psalm 19:14*

6

Best Friends

A friend loves you all the time.

Proverbs 17:17 ICB

L asting relationships are built upon love *and* friendship. What is a friend? The dictionary defines the word friend as "a person who is attached to another by feelings of affection or personal regard." This definition is accurate, as far as it goes, but when we examine the deeper meaning of friendship, especially as it applies to our loved ones, so many more descriptors apply: trustworthiness, loyalty, helpfulness, kindness, understanding, forgiveness, encouragement, humor, and cheerfulness, to mention but a few.

Is your spouse your best friend? Prayerfully this is the case. If so, you are immensely blessed by God. *Never* take this gift for granted. As you journey through the day, remember the important role that friendship plays in your marriage . . . and have fun accordingly!

Nothing bonds me closer to my husband than
interceding for him. If I sense my passion waning
or my emotions sagging, if I find myself pulling back
from the demands of marriage, I pray—for my husband.

Joni Eareckson Tada

The institution of marriage has been a sacred bond
of fidelity between a man and a woman in every culture
throughout recorded history. The pledge of loyalty
and mutual support represented by marriage vows
is a promise of commitment that extends
to every aspect of life.

James Dobson

The truth of the Gospel is intended to free us
to love God and others with our whole heart.

John Eldredge

Affection is responsible for nine-tenths
of whatever solid and durable happiness
there is in our natural lives.

C. S. Lewis

We long to find someone who has been where
we've been, who shares our fragile skies,
who sees our sunsets with the same shades of blue.

Beth Moore

*Beloved, if God so loved us,
we also ought to love one another.*

1 John 4:11 NKJV

∼ A Prayer ∼

Thank You Lord, for the gifts of friendship and love.
When friendship and love work together,
we are blessed beyond words. For these precious gifts,
we praise You, Father, now and forever.
Amen

∼ More Verses to Consider ∼

*Philippians 1:3
Proverbs 27:17
Psalm 133:1
John 15:14-15*

7

Learning
to Forgive

---

*Be kind and loving to each other, and forgive each other
just as God forgave you in Christ.*

Ephesians 4:32 NCV

I f we wish to build lasting relationships, we must learn how to forgive. Why? Because our loved ones are imperfect (as are we). How often must we forgive our spouses and our friends? More times than we can count; to do otherwise is to disobey God.

Are you easily frustrated by the inevitable imperfections of others? Are you easily angered? Do you sometimes hold on to feelings of bitterness and regret? If so, perhaps you need a refresher course in the art of forgiveness.

Perhaps granting forgiveness is hard for you. If so, you are not alone. Genuine, lasting forgiveness is often difficult to achieve—difficult but not impossible. Thankfully, with God's help, all things are possible, and that includes forgiveness. But, even though God is willing to help, He expects you to do some of the work.

If there exists even one person, alive or dead, whom you have not forgiven (and that includes yourself and, of course, your spouse), follow God's commandment and His will for your life: forgive. Bitterness, anger, and regret are not part of God's plan for your life. Forgiveness is.

Forgiveness is the precondition of love.

Catherine Marshall

When God tells us to love our enemies, he gives,
along with the command, the love itself.

Corrie ten Boom

Give me such love for God and men
as will blot out all hatred and bitterness.

Dietrich Bonhoeffer

Looking back over my life, all I can see is mercy
and grace written in large letters everywhere.
May God help me have the same kind of heart
toward those who wound or offend me.

Jim Cymbala

God loves you, and He yearns for you to turn away
from the path of evil. You need His forgiveness,
and you need Him to come into your life
and remake you from within.

Billy Graham

For if you forgive men when they sin against you,
your heavenly Father will also forgive you.
But if you do not forgive men their sins,
your Father will not forgive your sins.

Matthew 6:14-15 NIV

A Prayer

Lord, forgiveness is Your commandment,
and we know that we need to forgive others just as
You have forgiven us. Keep us mindful, Father,
that we are never fully liberated until we have been
freed from the chains of bitterness—and that You offer
us that freedom through Your Son, Christ Jesus.
Amen

More Verses to Consider

Romans 12:19
Psalm 103:3
Matthew 7:3-5
Matthew 18:21-22

8

Building Trust

Good people will be guided by honesty.

Proverbs 11:3 ICB

Lasting relationships are built upon a foundation of honesty and trust. It has been said on many occasions that honesty is *the best* policy. For believers, it is far more important to note that honesty is *God's* policy. And, if we are to be servants worthy of our Savior, Jesus Christ, we must be honest and forthright in all our communications with *all* people, starting with our loved ones.

Sometimes, honesty is difficult; sometimes, honesty is painful; sometimes, honesty makes us feel uncomfortable. Despite these temporary feelings of discomfort, we must make honesty the hallmark of all our relationships; otherwise, we invite needless suffering into our own lives and into the lives of those we love.

Sometime soon, perhaps even today, you will be tempted to bend the truth or perhaps even to break it. Resist that temptation. Truth is God's way…and it must be *your* way, too.

The single most important element in
any human relationship is honesty—with oneself,
with God, and with others.

Catherine Marshall

Honesty has a beautiful and refreshing
simplicity about it. No ulterior motives.
No hidden meanings. As honesty and integrity
characterize our lives, there will be
no need to manipulate others.

Charles Swindoll

Integrity is not a given factor in everyone's life.
It is a result of self-discipline, inner trust,
and a decision to be relentlessly honest
in all situations in our lives.

John Maxwell

God doesn't expect you to be perfect,
but he does insist on complete honesty.

Rick Warren

For God so loved the world that He gave
His only begotten Son, that whoever believes in Him
should not perish but have everlasting life.

John 3:16 NKJV

A Prayer

Dear Lord, You command Your children to walk
in truth. Let us follow Your commandment.
Give us the courage to speak honestly, and let us
walk righteously with You so that others might see
Your eternal truth reflected in our words and our deeds.
Amen

More Verses to Consider

John 15:13
Romans 5:8
1 Corinthians 13:4-7
Colossians 3:14

9

With a Spirit of Cooperation

*Behold, how good and how pleasant it is
for brethren to dwell together in unity!*

Psalm 133:1 NKJV

H ave you and your loved one learned the fine art of cooperation? If so, you have learned the wisdom of "give and take," not the foolishness of "me first." Cooperation is the art of compromising on little things while keeping your eye on the big thing: your relationship.

Cooperative relationships grow and flourish over time. But, when couples fail to cooperate, they unintentionally sow seeds of dissatisfaction and disharmony.

If you're like most of us, you're probably a little bit headstrong: you probably want most things done in a fashion resembling the popular song "My Way." But, if you are observant, you will notice that those people who always insist upon "my way or the highway" usually end up with "the highway."

A better strategy for all concerned is to abandon the search for "my way" and search instead for "our way." That tune has a far happier ending.

The Christian way of life lends stability
to marriage because its principles and values
naturally produce harmony.

James Dobson

That's what I love about serving God. In His eyes,
we are all on the same playing field. We all start
at square one. No one has it better than the other,
or possesses unfair advantage.

Joni Eareckson Tada

If Jesus is the preeminent One in our lives,
then we will love each other, submit to each other,
and treat one another fairly in the Lord.

Warren Wiersbe

If doing a good act in public will excite others
to do more good, then "Let your Light shine to all."
Miss no opportunity to do good.

John Wesley

Cooperation is a two-way street,
but for too many couples,
it's the road less traveled.

Marie T. Freeman

And they, continuing daily with one accord in the temple,
and breaking bread from house to house, did eat their meat
with gladness and singleness of heart, praising God,
and having favor with all the people. And the Lord added
to the church daily such as should be saved.

Acts 2:46-47 KJV

❧ A Prayer ❧

Lord, so much more can be accomplished
when we join together to fulfill our common goals
and desires. As we seek to fulfill Your will for our lives,
let us also join with others to accomplish
Your greater good for our families, for our communities,
for our nation, and for our world.

Amen

❧ More Verses to Consider ❧

Nehemiah 4:6
1 Corinthians 3:8-9
Mark 3:24-25

10

The Power of Patience

I waited patiently for the LORD;
And He inclined to me, And heard my cry.

Psalm 40:1 NKJV

L oving relationships inevitably require patience . . . and lots of it! We live in an imperfect world inhabited by imperfect people, and we need to be patient with everybody, *especially* those we love. Most of us, however, are perfectly willing to be patient with our spouses just as long as things happen RIGHT NOW! Or sooner.

Ephesians 4:2 instructs us, "Be completely humble and gentle; be patient, bearing with one another in love" (NIV). But, for most of us, "bearing with one another" is difficult. Why? Because we are fallible human beings, sometimes quick to anger and sometimes slow to forgive.

The next time you find *your* patience tested to the limit, remember that the world unfolds according to God's timetable, not ours. Sometimes, we must wait patiently for our loved ones, and sometimes we must wait patiently for God. And that's as it should be. After all, think how patient God has been with us.

Teach us, O Lord, the disciplines of patience,
for to wait is often harder than to work.

Peter Marshall

If only we could be as patient with other people
as God is with us!

Jim Gallery

The times we find ourselves having to wait
on others may be the perfect opportunities
to train ourselves to wait on the Lord.

Joni Eareckson Tada

Patience is the companion of wisdom.

St. Augustine

A patient heart is better than a tranquilizer.

Marie T. Freeman

We urge you, brethren, admonish the unruly,
encourage the fainthearted, help the weak,
be patient with everyone.

1 *Thessalonians* 5:14 NASB

A Prayer

Heavenly Father, give us patience. Let us live
according to Your plan and according to Your timetable.
When we are hurried, slow us down. When we become
impatient with others, give us empathy. When we are
frustrated by the demands of the day, give us peace.
Today, let us be patient Christians, Dear Lord,
as we trust in You and in Your master plan for our lives.
Amen

More Verses to Consider

2 Timothy 2:24
Colossians 3:12
James 1:3-4
Lamentations 3:25-26

11

The Words We Speak

Watch the way you talk. Let nothing foul or dirty come out of your mouth. Say only what helps, each word a gift.

Ephesians 4:29 MSG

All too often, we underestimate the importance of the words we speak. Whether we realize it or not, our words carry great weight and great power, especially when we are addressing our loved ones.

The Bible reminds us that "Reckless words pierce like a sword, but the tongue of the wise brings healing" (Proverbs 12:18 NIV). And Christ taught that "Out of the abundance of the heart the mouth speaks" (Matthew 12:34 NKJV).

Does the "abundance of your heart" produce a continuing flow of uplifting words for your loved one? And do you express those feelings many times each day? You should.

When you're angry, do you reign in your tongue? Proverbs 29:11 teaches, "A fool gives full vent to his anger, but a wise man keeps himself under control" (NIV).

So, if you'd like to build a better marriage—and if you'd like to *keep* building it day by day—think before you speak. Avoid angry outbursts. Refrain from constant criticism. Terminate tantrums. Negate negativism. Cease from being cynical. Instead, use Christ as your guide, and speak words of encouragement, hope, praise, and, above all, love—and speak them often.

Fill the heart with the love of Christ so that
only truth and purity can come out of the mouth.

Warren Wiersbe

The great test of a man's character is his tongue.

Oswald Chambers

I still believe we ought to talk about Jesus.
The old country doctor of my boyhood days
always began his examination by saying,
"Let me see your tongue."
That's a good way to check a Christian:
the tongue test. Let's hear what he is talking about.

Vance Havner

The things that we feel most deeply we ought to
learn to be silent about, at least until
we have talked them over thoroughly with God.

Elisabeth Elliot

Words. Do you fully understand their power?
Can any of us really grasp the mighty force behind
the things we say? Do we stop and think
before we speak, considering the potency
of the words we utter?

Joni Eareckson Tada

To everything there is a season . . .
a time to keep silence, and a time to speak.

Ecclesiastes 3:1,7 KJV

A Prayer

Dear Lord, make our words pleasing to You.
Let us be a source of encouragement to each other
as we share a message of faith and assurance with
the world. Today, we will honor You, Father,
by choosing our words carefully, thoughtfully,
and lovingly.
Amen

More Verses to Consider

James 1:26
Luke 12:3
Matthew 12:34
Proverbs 10:14

12

Making Right Choices

I have set before you life and death, blessings and curses.
Now choose life, so that you and your children may live
*and that you may love the L*ORD *your God,*
listen to his voice, and hold fast to him.

Deuteronomy 30:19-20 NIV

---

hen it comes to the choices you make, it's not very complicated: the quality of your choices will, to a great extent, determine the quality of your marriage.

Each day, we make countless decisions that can bring us closer to God *and* to our loved ones...*or not.* When we live according to God's commandments, we earn for ourselves the abundance and peace that He intends for our lives. But, when we turn our backs upon God by disobeying Him, we bring needless suffering upon ourselves and upon our families.

Do you seek spiritual abundance that can be yours through the person of God's only begotten Son? Then you must make right choices, starting with the choice to invite Christ to reign over your actions and your relationships. When you do, you will receive untold blessings for yourself *and* for your loved ones—blessings not only for this day, but also for all eternity.

Commitment to His lordship on Easter, at revivals,
or even every Sunday is not enough. We must choose
this day—and every day—whom we will serve.
This deliberate act of the will is the inevitable choice
between habitual fellowship and habitual failure.

Beth Moore

Life is a series of choices between
the bad, the good, and the best.
Everything depends on how we choose.

Vance Havner

We are either the masters or the victims of our attitudes.
It is a matter of personal choice. Who we are today
is the result of choices we made yesterday.
Tomorrow, we will become what we choose today.
To change means to choose to change.

John Maxwell

I could go through this day oblivious to the miracles
all around me or I could tune in and "enjoy."

Gloria Gaither

Faith is not a feeling; it is action. It is a willed choice.

Elisabeth Elliot

*But Daniel purposed in his heart that
he would not defile himself . . . .*

Daniel 1:8 KJV

A Prayer

Dear Lord, help us to make choices that are pleasing
to You. Help us to be honest, patient, and kind.
And above all, help us to follow the teachings of Jesus,
not just today, but every day.

Amen

More Verses to Consider

James 1:22
1 Peter 1:13-15
1 Thessalonians 2:12

13

A Willingness to Solve Problems

*People who do what is right may have many problems,
but the Lord will solve them all.*

Psalm 34:19 NCV

From time to time, all of us face problems, disappointments, heartaches, and loss. Old Man Trouble pays periodic visits to each of us; none of us are exempt, and neither are our marriages. When we are troubled, God stands ready and willing to protect us. Our responsibility, of course, is to ask for His healing touch. When we call upon Him in heartfelt prayer, He will answer—in His own time and in accordance with His own perfect plan.

When we encounter problems or misunderstandings in our relationships, we must work to heal those problems sooner rather than later. Marital problems, like all problems, are most easily solved when they are new and small. That's why wise couples do the hard work of addressing their problems honestly, forthrightly, and *quickly* (even when they might prefer to downplay their difficulties or ignore those difficulties altogether).

Ignoring problems instead of fixing them is tempting but irresponsible. After all, if *we* won't solve our problems, who will? Or should?

In summary, the hallmark of a healthy marriage is not *the absence* of problems, but a *willingness to solve* those problems *now*. May you live—and love—accordingly.

Both a good marriage and a bad marriage have
moments of struggle, but in a healthy relationship,
the husband and wife search for answers and areas
of agreement because they love each other.

James Dobson

Often, in the midst of great problems,
we stop short of the real blessing God has for us,
which is a fresh vision of who He is.

Anne Graham Lotz

We are all faced with a series of great opportunities,
brilliantly disguised as unsolvable problems.
Unsolvable without God's wisdom, that is.

Charles Swindoll

Faith does not eliminate problems.
Faith keeps you in a trusting relationship with God
in the midst of your problems.

Henry Blackaby

Don't wait for the "perfect" time to solve your problems.
The "perfect" time to solve them is now.

Marie T. Freeman

For whatever is born of God overcomes the world.
And this is the victory that has overcome the world—
our faith.

1 John 5:4 NKJV

⇜ A Prayer ⇝

Heavenly Father, You are our strength and our refuge.
As we journey through this day, we know that we
will encounter problems. Remind us that
You enable us to solve all the struggles we face
and that nothing is impossible for You.
Amen

⇜ More Verses to Consider ⇝

2 Corinthians 4:8
2 Samuel 22:7
Hebrews 12:11
James 1:2-3

14

Sharing the Joy

Weeping may endure for a night,
but joy cometh in the morning.

Psalm 30:5 KJV

---

hrist made it clear to His followers: He intended that His joy would become their joy. And it still holds true today: Christ intends that His believers share His love with joy in their hearts. Yet sometimes, amid the inevitable hustle and bustle of life-here-on-earth, we can forfeit—albeit temporarily—the joy of Christ as we wrestle with the challenges of daily living.

Joy is an important part of healthy Christian relationships. Joyful believers tend to form joyful relationships, and that is exactly what God intends.

C. H. Spurgeon, the renowned 19th century English clergymen, advised, "The Lord is glad to open the gate to every knocking soul. It opens very freely; its hinges are not rusted; no bolts secure it. Have faith and enter at this moment through holy courage. If you knock with a heavy heart, you shall yet sing with joy of spirit. Never be discouraged!"

Are you doing your best to live each day as a joyful servant of Christ? And, are you inviting your spouse to join in the celebration? Hopefully so. After all, few things in life are more wonderful to behold than the joining together of two joyful believers. So now, with no further ado, thank God for your marriage, and let the celebration begin!

Christ is not only a remedy for your weariness
and trouble, but he will give you an abundance of
the contrary: joy and delight. They who come to Christ
do not only come to a resting-place after they have been
wandering in a wilderness, but they come to
a banqueting-house where they may rest, and where
they may feast. They may cease from their former
troubles and toils, and they may enter upon a course
of delights and spiritual joys.

Jonathan Edwards

The Christian should be an alleluia from head to foot!

St. Augustine

I choose joy. I will refuse the temptation to be cynical;
cynicism is the tool of a lazy thinker. I will refuse to see
people as anything less than human beings, created by
God. I will refuse to see any problem as anything
less than an opportunity to see God.

Max Lucado

Marriage should be many hours of joy interrupted by
an occasional minute or two of frustration—
not the other way around.

Marie T. Freeman

May the God of hope fill you with all joy and peace
as you trust in him, so that you may overflow
with hope by the power of the Holy Spirit.

Romans 15:13 NIV

A Prayer

Dear Lord, You have given us so many blessings;
let us celebrate Your gifts. Make us thankful, loving,
responsible, and wise. We praise You, Father,
for the gift of Your Son and for the priceless gift
of salvation. Make us joyful Christians,
make us worthy examples to others,
and make us dutiful servants to You,
now and forever.
Amen

More Verses to Consider

Psalm 51:8
Psalm 47:1
Philippians 4:4
John 15:11

15

Beyond Anger

---

*Do not let the sun go down on your anger,
and do not give the devil an opportunity.*

Ephesians 4:26-27 NASB

A nger is a natural human emotion that is sometimes necessary and appropriate. Even Jesus became angry when confronted with the moneychangers in the temple (Matthew 21:12). Righteous indignation is an appropriate response to evil, but God does not intend that anger should rule our lives. And, just as importantly, God does not intend that anger should rule our marriages. He instructs us to turn *away* from anger whenever possible and forgive others just as we seek forgiveness for ourselves. And forgiveness, like so many other things, starts at home.

Life is full of frustrations: some great and some small. Most of our frustrations are of the more mundane variety. As long as we live, we will inevitably face countless opportunities to lose our tempers over small, relatively insignificant events: a traffic jam, a spilled cup of coffee, an inconsiderate comment, a forgotten promise.

When *you* are tempted to lose *your* temper over the minor inconveniences of life, don't. And while you're at it, don't bring anger into the sanctity of your marriage. Turn away from anger and turn instead to God. When you do, you'll honor Him by sharing His gift: the gift of peace. And what a beautiful gift it is.

Anger is the noise of the soul; the unseen irritant
of the heart; the relentless invader of silence.

Max Lucado

What is hatred, after all, other than anger that
was allowed to remain, that has become ingrained
and deep-rooted? What was anger when it was fresh
becomes hatred when it is aged.

St. Augustine

When you strike out in anger, you may miss
the other person, but you will always hit yourself.

Jim Gallery

Anger breeds remorse in the heart, discord in the home,
bitterness in the community, and confusion in the state.

Billy Graham

Bitterness and anger, usually over trivial things,
make havoc of homes, churches, and friendships.

Warren Wiersbe

Wise men turn away anger.

Proverbs 29:8 NASB

∽ A Prayer ∽

Lord, sometimes we are quick to anger
and slow to forgive. But we know, Lord,
that You seek abundance and peace for our lives.
Forgiveness is Your commandment; empower us
to follow the example of Your Son Jesus who forgave
His persecutors. As we turn away from anger,
we claim the peace that You intend for our lives.
Amen

∽ More Verses to Consider ∽

Psalm 4:4
Proverbs 29:11
Proverbs 20:3
Proverbs 14:29

16

The Power of Encouraging Words

Good people's words will help many others.

Proverbs 10:21 NCV

Marriage is a team sport, and all of us need occasional pats on the back from our teammate. In the Book of Proverbs, we read that, "A word aptly spoken is like apples of gold in settings of silver" (25:11 NIV). This verse reminds us that the words we speak can and should be beautiful offerings to those we love.

All of us have the power to enrich the lives of our loved ones. Sometimes, when we feel uplifted and secure, we find it easy to speak words of encouragement and hope. Other times, when we are discouraged or tired, we can scarcely summon the energy to uplift ourselves, much less anyone else. But, as loving Christians, our obligation is clear: we must always measure our words carefully as we use them to benefit others and to glorify our Father in heaven.

God intends that we speak words of kindness, wisdom, and truth, no matter our circumstances, no matter our emotions. When we do, we share a priceless gift with our loved ones, and we give glory to the One who gave His life for us. As believers, we must do no less.

A lot of people have gone further
than they thought they could
because someone else thought they could.

Zig Ziglar

God of our life, there are days when the burdens
we carry chafe our shoulders and weigh us down;
when the road seems dreary and endless, the skies gray
and threatening; when our lives have no music in them,
and our hearts are lonely, and our souls have
lost their courage. Flood the path with light,
run our eyes to where the skies are full of promise;
tune our hearts to brave music; give us the sense
of comradeship with heroes and saints of every age;
and so quicken our spirits that we may be able
to encourage the souls of all who journey with us on
the road of life, to Your honor and glory.

St. Augustine

Encouragement starts at home,
but it should never end there.

Marie T. Freeman

People who inspire others are those who see
invisible bridges at the end of dead-end streets.

Charles Swindoll

*Let's see how inventive we can be in encouraging love
and helping out, not avoiding worshipping together
as some do but spurring each other on.*

Hebrews 10:24-25 MSG

∽ A Prayer ∽

Dear Heavenly Father, because we are Your children,
we are blessed. You have loved us eternally,
cared for us faithfully, and saved us through
the gift of Your Son Jesus. Just as You have lifted us up,
Lord, we will seek to lift each other up in a spirit
of encouragement, optimism, and hope.
Amen

∽ More Verses to Consider ∽

2 Corinthians 13:11
1 Thessalonians 5:14
Hebrews 3:13
Romans 14:19

Love Requires Effort

So prepare your minds for service and have self-control.

1 Peter 1:13 NCV

Building a lasting relationship requires effort, which is perfectly okay with God. God has created a world in which diligence is rewarded and sloth is not. So, if you sincerely want to build a loving relationship that stands the test of time, you must be willing to work at it. Period.

The work of building a marriage requires heaping helpings of consideration, cooperation, self-sacrifice, discipline, empathy, patience, prayer, and perseverance. If that sounds like lots of work, it is—but the rewards are worth it.

God did not create you for a life of mediocrity, and He does not intend that your marriage be "average." He created you and your spouse for far greater things. Reaching for greater things usually requires effort, and so it is with your marriage. Success doesn't come easily, which is just fine with God. After all, He knows that you're up to the task, and He has big plans for you *and* your marriage. Very big plans…

True willpower and courage are not on the battlefield,
but in everyday conquests over our inertia,
laziness, and boredom.

D. L. Moody

If one examines the secret behind a championship
football team, a magnificent orchestra,
or a successful business,
the principal ingredient is invariably discipline.

James Dobson

The alternative to discipline is disaster.

Vance Havner

The effective Christians of history have been men
and women of great personal discipline—
mental discipline, discipline of the body,
discipline of the tongue, and discipline of the emotion.

Billy Graham

The secret of a happy life is to delight in duty.
When duty becomes delight,
then burdens become blessings.

Warren Wiersbe

Discipline yourself for the purpose of godliness.

1 Timothy 4:7 NASB

⟶ A Prayer ⟵

Lord, we know that You desire a bountiful harvest for us.
But, You have instructed us that we must sow before
we reap, not after. Help us, Lord, to sow the seeds of
Your abundance everywhere we go, starting at home.
And, at the proper time, let us reap the harvest that
is found in Your will for our lives.

Amen

⟶ More Verses to Consider ⟵

Proverbs 1:7
Proverbs 16:32
Titus 1:7-8
1 Corinthians 9:24-27

18

Taking Time to Laugh

There is a time for everything, and a season
for every activity under heaven . . .
a time to weep and a time to laugh,
a time to mourn and a time to dance . . . .

Ecclesiastes 3:1,4 NIV

The old saying is true: "He who laughs, lasts." And the same can be said for couples. Laughter is not only tonic for our souls, it is also medicine for our marriages. But sometimes, amid the stresses of the day, we forget to take our medicine. Instead of viewing our lives with a mixture of optimism and humor, we begin to take things a little too seriously by allowing worries and distractions to rob us of the joy that God intends for our lives.

So the next time you and your spouse begin to dwell upon the negatives of life, refocus your attention to things positive. The next time you find yourself falling prey to the blight of pessimism, stop yourself and turn your thoughts around. And, if you see your glass as "half-empty," rest assured that your spiritual vision is impaired. With God, your glass is never half-empty. With God as your protector and Christ as your Savior, your glass is filled to the brim and overflowing...forever.

Today, as a gift to yourself and to your beloved, approach life with a smile on your lips and hope in your heart. And laugh every chance you get. After all, God created laughter for a reason...and Father indeed knows best. So laugh often and, more importantly, laugh *together*!

It is often just as sacred to laugh as it is to pray.
Charles Swindoll

It is pleasing to the dear God whenever thou rejoicest
or laughest from the bottom of thy heart.
Martin Luther

There is nothing that rejuvenates the parched,
delicate spirits of children faster than when
a lighthearted spirit pervades the home
and laughter fills its halls.
James Dobson

Humor ought to be consecrated and used
for the cause of Christ.
C. H. Spurgeon

God has charged Himself with full responsibility
for our eternal happiness and stands ready to take over
the management of our lives the moment
we turn in faith to Him.
A. W. Tozer

Nehemiah said, "Go and enjoy choice food and sweet drinks,
and send some to those who have nothing prepared.
This day is sacred to our Lord. Do not grieve,
for the joy of the LORD is your strength."

Nehemiah 8:10 NIV

A Prayer

Lord, when we begin to take ourselves or our lives
too seriously, let us laugh. When we rush from place
to place, slow us down, Lord, and let us laugh.
Put a smile on our faces, Dear Lord, and let us share
that smile with all who cross our paths . . .
and let us laugh.
Amen

More Verses to Consider

Proverbs 15:13
Proverbs 17:22
Psalm 47:1
Psalm 98:4-6

19

Sharing Hopes and Dreams

*This hope we have as an anchor of the soul,
a hope both sure and steadfast.*

Hebrews 6:19 NASB

Are you willing to share your hopes and dreams? And, are you willing to entertain the possibility that God has big plans in store for you and your spouse? Hopefully so. Yet sometimes, especially if you've recently experienced a life-altering disappointment, you may find it difficult to envision a brighter future for yourself or your family. If so, it's time to reconsider your own capabilities—and God's.

Your heavenly Father created you and yours with unique gifts and untapped talents; your job is to tap those talents and use them for God's purposes.

It takes courage to dream big dreams and even more courage to share them. You will discover that kind of courage when you do three things: accept the past, trust God to handle the future, and make the most of the time He has given you today. Nothing is too difficult for God, and no dreams are too big for Him—not even yours. So start living—and dreaming—accordingly.

Dreams are wonderful things to share. Have you shared yours lately? Hopefully you have. But if you've been hesitant to give voice to your hopes and dreams, remember this: dreaming works best when it's a team sport.

Everything that is done in the world is done by hope.

Martin Luther

You cannot out-dream God.

John Eldredge

Sometimes our dreams were so big
that it took two people to dream them.

Marie T. Freeman

When you accept the fact that sometimes seasons
are dry and times are hard and that God is in control
of both, you will discover a sense of divine refuge
because the hope then is in God and not in yourself.

Charles Swindoll

The essence of optimism is that it takes no account
of the present, but it is a source of inspiration,
of vitality, and of hope. Where others have resigned,
it enables a man to hold his head high, to claim
the future for himself, and not abandon it to his enemy.

Dietrich Bonhoeffer

*"I say this because I know what I am planning for you," says
the Lord. "I have good plans for you, not plans to hurt you.
I will give you hope and a good future."*

Jeremiah 29:11 NCV

⟶ A Prayer ⟵

Dear Lord, give us the courage to dream
and the faithfulness to trust in Your perfect plan.
When we are worried or weary, give us strength
for today and hope for tomorrow. Keep us mindful
of Your infinite love, Your healing power,
and Your glorious plans for us
today, tomorrow, and forever.
Amen

⟶ More Verses to Consider ⟵

Lamentations 3:25-26
Proverbs 24:14
Psalm 146:5
Psalm 38:15

20

The Importance of Renewal

Inwardly we are being renewed day by day.
2 Corinthians 4:16 NIV

E ven the most inspired Christians can, from time to time, find themselves running on empty. The demands of daily life can drain us of our strength and rob us of the joy that is rightfully ours in Christ. When we find ourselves tired, discouraged, or worse, there is a source from which we can draw the power needed to recharge our spiritual batteries. That source is God.

God is in the business of making all things new, including marriages. When we feel the strains of everyday living tugging at the seams of our hearts, God is always able to renew us *if* we join together and ask Him to do so. Our obligation is to ask.

Are you and your spouse tired or troubled? Turn your hearts toward God in prayer. Are you weak or worried? Take the time—or, more accurately, make the time—to delve deeply into God's Holy Word. Are you spiritually depleted? Call upon fellow believers to support you, and call upon Christ to renew your marriage and your lives. When you do, you'll discover that the Creator of the universe stands ready to restore your strength, your relationship, and your love.

Christ came when all things were growing old.
He made them new.

St. Augustine

Repentance removes old sins and wrong attitudes,
and it opens the way for the Holy Spirit
to restore our spiritual health.

Shirley Dobson

God is not running an antique shop!
He is making all things new!

Vance Havner

The amazing thing about Jesus is that
He doesn't just patch up our lives, He gives us
a brand new sheet, a clean slate to start over, all new.

Gloria Gaither

Father, for this day, renew within me
the gift of the Holy Spirit.

Andrew Murray

*Therefore if anyone is in Christ,
he is a new creature; the old things passed away;
behold, new things have come.*

2 Corinthians 5:17 HCSB

A Prayer

Heavenly Father, sometimes we are troubled,
and sometimes we grow weary. When we are weak,
Lord, give us strength. When we are discouraged,
renew us. When we are fearful, let us feel
Your healing touch. Let us always trust in
Your promises, Lord, and let us draw strength from
those promises and from Your unending love.
Amen

More Verses to Consider

*Ezekiel 36:26
Isaiah 40:28–31
Matthew 11:28–30
Proverbs 24:16*

21

Celebrating Life and Love

Your life and your marriage are gifts from God: celebrate them and give thanks. When you celebrate the gifts of life and love, your thankful heart will serve as a powerful blessing to your loved ones.

Every good gift comes from God. As believers who have been saved by a risen Christ, we owe unending thanksgiving to our Heavenly Father. Yet sometimes, amid the crush of everyday living, we simply don't stop long enough to pause and thank our Creator for His countless blessings. As Christians, we are blessed beyond measure. Thus, thanksgiving should become a habit, a regular part of our daily routines.

Christian believers can face the inevitable challenges of married life armed with the joy of Christ and the promise of salvation. So whatever this day holds for you, begin it and end it with God as your partner and Christ as your Savior. And throughout the day, give thanks to the One who created you and saved you. Place God squarely at the center of your marriage and your life. Then celebrate! God's love for you is infinite. Accept it joyously and be thankful.

Life is a glorious opportunity.

Billy Graham

When we invite Jesus into our lives,
we experience life in the fullest, most vital sense.

Catherine Marshall

The life of faith is a daily exploration of
the constant and countless ways in which
God's grace and love are experienced.

Eugene Peterson

Life is not a problem to be solved;
it is an adventure to be lived.

John Eldredge

God, forgive us in an hour like this, that we have been
dry Christians, preaching a dynamite Gospel
while living firecracker lives.

Vance Havner

> *For whoever finds me finds life*
> *and receives favor from the* LORD.

Proverbs 8:35 NIV

A Prayer

Lord, You are the Giver of all Life, and You have created
us to have fellowship with You. Let us live our lives
in ways that are pleasing to You. We will celebrate
together, Father, and we will give thanks for
Your blessings today *and* throughout all eternity.
Amen

More Verses to Consider

Philippians 1:21
Psalm 16:11
Matthew 6:27
Matthew 16:24-25

22

Keeping Possessions in Perspective

---

*A man's life does not consist in
the abundance of his possessions.*

Luke 12:15 NIV

How important are our material possessions? Not as important as we might think. In the life of committed Christians, material possessions should play a rather small role, but sometimes, we allow the things that we own to take control of our lives. When we do, we suffer.

Too many marriages are weighted down by endless concerns about money and possessions. Too many couples mistakenly focus their thoughts and energies on newer cars, better clothes, and bigger houses. The results of these misplaced priorities are always unfortunate, and sometimes tragic.

Certainly we all need the basic necessities of life, but once we meet those needs for our families and ourselves, the piling up of possessions creates more problems than it solves. Our real riches are not of this world: we are never *really* rich until we are rich in spirit.

Do you find yourself wrapped up in the concerns of the material world? If so, it's time for you and your spouse to sit down and have a heart-to-heart talk about "stuff." When you do, you should reorder your priorities by turning *away* from materialism and *back* to God. Then, you can begin storing up riches that will endure throughout eternity: the spiritual kind.

Hold everything earthly with a loose hand,
but grasp eternal things with a deathlike grip.

C. H. Spurgeon

I have held many things in my hands,
and I have lost them all;
but whatever I have placed in God's hands,
that I still possess.

Corrie ten Boom

He is no fool who gives what he cannot keep
to gain what he cannot lose.

Jim Elliot

What we possess often possesses us—
we are possessed by possessions.

Oswald Chambers

Therefore I tell you, do not worry about your life,
what you will eat or drink; or about your body,
what you will wear. Is not life more important than food,
and the body more important than clothes? Look at the birds
of the air; they do not sow or reap or store away in barns,
and yet your heavenly Father feeds them.
Are you not much more valuable than they?

Matthew 6:25-26 NIV

A Prayer

Lord, our greatest possession is our relationship
with You through Jesus Christ. You have promised
that, when we first seek Your kingdom and
Your righteousness, You will give us whatever we need.
Let us trust You completely, Lord, for our needs,
both material and spiritual, this day and always.
Amen

More Verses to Consider

1 Corinthians 2:9
Matthew 6:19-21
1 Timothy 6:6–8
Hebrews 13:5

23

The Joys of
Family Life

---

*Choose for yourselves this day whom you will serve . . .
as for me and my household, we will serve the LORD.*

Joshua 24:15 NIV

In a world filled with countless obligations and frequent frustrations, we may be tempted to take our families for granted. But God intends otherwise.

Our families are precious gifts from our Father in heaven. If we are to be the righteous men and women that God intends, we must care for our loved ones by making time for them, even when the demands of the day are great.

Undeniably, these are difficult days for Christian households: never have distractions and temptations been greater. But, thankfully, God is bigger than all our challenges.

No family is perfect, and neither is yours. But, despite the inevitable challenges, obligations, and hurt feelings of family life, your clan is God's blessing to you. That little band of men, women, kids, and babies is a priceless treasure on temporary loan from the Father above. Give thanks to the Giver for the gift of family… and act accordingly.

Apart from religious influence, the family
is the most important influence on society.

Billy Graham

There is so much compassion and understanding
that is gained when we've experienced God's grace
firsthand within our own families.

Lisa Whelchel

The only true source of meaning in life is found
in love for God and his son Jesus Christ,
and love for mankind,
beginning with our own families.

James Dobson

A man ought to live so that everybody knows
he is a Christian, and most of all,
his family ought to know.

D. L. Moody

. . . these should learn first of all to put their religion into practice by caring for their own family . . . .

1 Timothy 5:4 NIV

A Prayer

Dear Lord, we are part of Your family, and we praise
You for Your gifts and for Your love. You have also
blessed us with our own earthly family, and we pray for
them, that they might be protected and blessed by You.
Let us show love and acceptance for our family,
Lord, so that through us, they might come
to know You and to love You.

Amen

More Verses to Consider

Proverbs 3:33
Psalm 127:1
Romans 12:9–10

24

Growing
Together

---

*Long for the pure milk of the word,
so that by it you may grow in respect to salvation.*

1 Peter 2:2 NASB

Christian marriage can and should be a lifelong journey toward spiritual maturity and growth: as believers, we should never stop growing in the love and knowledge of our Savior.

When we cease to grow, either emotionally or spiritually, we do ourselves and our loved ones a profound disservice. But, if we study God's Word, if we obey His commandments, and if we live in the center of His will, we will not be "stagnant" believers; we will, instead, be growing Christians . . . and that's exactly what God wants for our lives.

Many of life's most important lessons are painful to learn. Thankfully, during times of heartbreak and hardship, God stands ready to protect us. As Psalm 46:1 promises, "God is our protection and our strength. He always helps in times of trouble" (NCV). In His own time and according to His master plan, God will heal us *if* we invite Him into our hearts.

Spiritual growth need not take place only in times of adversity. We must seek to grow in our knowledge and love of the Lord every day that we live. In those quiet moments when we open our hearts to God, the One who made us keeps remaking us. He gives us direction, perspective, wisdom, and courage. And, the appropriate moment to accept those spiritual gifts is always the present one.

Grow, dear friends, but grow, I beseech you,
in God's way, which is the only true way.

Hannah Whitall Smith

The main thing is not work for the Lord;
it is not suffering in the name of the Lord;
it is not witnessing to the Lord; it is not teaching
Sunday School for the Lord; it is not being responsible
for the sake of the Lord in the community; it is not
keeping the Ten Commandments; not loving your
neighbor; not observing the golden rule. "The chief end
of man is to glorify God and enjoy him forever."
Or, in the vocabulary of Psalm 134, "Bless the LORD."
All movements of discipleship arrive at a place where
joy is experienced. Every step of assent toward God
develops the capacity to enjoy. Not only is there,
increasingly, more to be enjoyed, there is steadily
the acquired ability to enjoy it.

Eugene Peterson

Transformation will begin in any life—in yours—when
you stand up and say: "I'm responsible for the kind of
person I am. I am what I've wanted to be. Now I've
changed my mind. I'm sorry for what I am and for what I
have done. I'm going to be different. God help me."

E. Stanley Jones

*But grow in the grace and knowledge of our Lord
and Savior Jesus Christ. To Him be the glory,
both now and to the day of eternity.*

2 Peter 3:18 NASB

A Prayer

Dear Lord, when we open ourselves to You,
we are blessed. We accept Your love and Your wisdom,
Father. Show us Your way, and deliver us from
the painful mistakes that we make when we stray from
Your commandments. Let us live according to
Your Word, and let us grow in our faith
every day that we live.
Amen

More Verses to Consider

Ephesians 3:18-19
Proverbs 3:5
Philippians 1:6
2 Timothy 3:14-15

25

When Times
Are Tough

LORD, help! they cried in their trouble,
and he saved them from their distress.

Psalm 107:13 NLT

L ife is a tapestry of good days and difficult days, with the good days predominating. When times are good, we are tempted to take our blessings for granted. But, when times are tough, we discover precisely what we're made of.

Every marriage, like every life, will encounter days of hardship and pain. It is only then that husbands and wives can discover precisely what *their marriage* is made of.

When we experience a deeply significant loss, we must learn (once again) to trust God *and* to trust those who love us most. When we do, we come to understand that our suffering carries with it great potential: the potential for intense personal growth *and* the potential to add depth and meaning to our relationships.

Are you and your spouse enduring tough times? If so, hold tight to each other and turn your hearts toward God. When you do, you may rest assured that the two of you—plus God—can handle anything that comes your way.

Often, in the midst of great problems,
we stop short of the real blessing God has for us,
which is a fresh vision of who He is.

Anne Graham Lotz

Life will be made or broken at the place
where we meet and deal with obstacles.

E. Stanley Jones

Faith does not eliminate problems.
Faith keeps you in a trusting relationship with God
in the midst of your problems.

Henry Blackaby

Let God's promises shine on your problems.

Corrie ten Boom

The happiest people in the world are not those
who have no problems, but the people who have learned
to live with those things that are less than perfect.

James Dobson

People who do what is right may have many problems,
but the Lord will solve them all.

Psalm 34:19 NCV

A Prayer

Lord, sometimes life is so difficult that we don't see hope
for the future. But with You, there is always hope.
Today, give us the courage to trust You completely.
You are our protector, dear Lord; we will praise You
and we will trust in the perfect wisdom of
Your plan for our lives.
Amen

More Verses to Consider

Romans 5:3-4
Psalm 9:10
Joshua 1:9
James 1:3-4

26

Worshiping Together

For it is written, "You shall worship the Lord your God,
and Him only you shall serve."

Matthew 4:10 NKJV

The old saying is familiar and true: "The family that prays together stays together." And, our world would be a far better place if more husbands and wives spent more time *praying together* and less time *drifting apart.*

We should never deceive ourselves: every marriage is based upon some form of worship. The question is not *whether* we worship, but *what* we worship. Some families choose to worship God. The result is a plentiful harvest of joy, peace, and abundance. Other families distance themselves from God by foolishly worshiping things of this earth such as fame, fortune, or personal gratification. To do so is a terrible mistake with eternal consequences.

Whenever we place our love for material possessions above our love for God—or when we yield to the countless temptations of this world—we find ourselves engaged in a struggle between good and evil, a clash between God and Satan. Our responses to these struggles have implications that echo throughout our families and throughout our communities. How can we ensure that we cast our lot with God? We do so, in part, by committing ourselves to the discipline of regular worship *with our families.*

Every day provides opportunities to put God where He belongs: at the center of our lives and our marriages. When we do so, we worship not just with our words, but also with deeds, and that's as it should be. For believers, God comes first. Always first.

I am of the opinion that we should not be concerned
about working for God until we have learned
the meaning and delight of worshipping Him.

A. W. Tozer

Praise Him! Praise Him! Tell of His excellent greatness.
Praise Him! Praise Him! Ever in joyful song!

Fanny Crosby

Worship is not taught from the pulpit.
It must be learned in the heart.

Jim Elliot

It's our privilege to not only raise our hands in worship
but also to combine the visible with the invisible
in a rising stream of praise and adoration
sent directly to our Father.

Shirley Dobson

Let this be your chief object in prayer, to realize
the presence of your heavenly Father.
Let your watchword be: Alone with God.

Andrew Murray

Don't fret or worry, Instead of worrying, pray.
Let petitions and praises shape your worries into prayers,
letting God know your concerns. Before you know it,
a sense of God's wholeness, everything coming together
for good, will come and settle you down.
It's wonderful what happens when
Christ displaces worry at the center of your life.

Philippians 4:6-7 MSG

❧ A Prayer ☙

Heavenly Father, let today and every day be a time
of worship. Let us worship You, not only with words and
deeds, but also with our hearts. In the quiet moments
of the day, we will praise You and thank You for
creating us, loving us, guiding us, and saving us.

Amen

❧ More Verses to Consider ☙

Psalm 95:1-2
Psalm 66:4
Philippians 2:9-11
John 4:23-24

27

Wisdom from God's Word

But if any of you lacks wisdom, let him ask of God,
who gives to all generously and without reproach,
and it will be given to him.

James 1:5 NASB

Wise Christian couples understand the transforming power of God's Holy Word. The Bible is unlike any other book. It is a priceless gift from our Creator, a tool that God intends for us to use in every aspect of our lives. And, it contains promises upon which we, as Christians, can and must depend.

Jonathan Edwards advised, "Be assiduous in reading the Holy Scriptures. This is the fountain whence all knowledge in divinity must be derived. Therefore let not this treasure lie by you neglected." God's Holy Word is, indeed, a priceless, one-of-a-kind treasure. We should handle it with care, but more importantly, we should handle it every day.

Would you like to energize your marriage and your life? Then open your Bible and read it with a focused mind *and* an open heart. And remember: God has given you the Bible for the purpose of knowing His promises, His power, His commandments, His wisdom, His love, and His Son. As you study God's teachings and apply them to your life, you will live by the Word that shall never pass away.

Wisdom is knowledge applied.
Head knowledge is useless on the battlefield.
Knowledge stamped on the heart makes one wise.

Beth Moore

Don't expect wisdom to come into your life like
great chunks of rock on a conveyor belt.
Wisdom comes privately from God as a byproduct
of right decisions, godly reactions, and the application
of spiritual principles to daily circumstances.

Charles Swindoll

The fruit of wisdom is Christlikeness, peace, humility,
and love. And, the root of it is faith in Christ
as the manifested wisdom of God.

J. I. Packer

Knowledge can be found in books or in school.
Wisdom, on the other hand, starts with God . . .
and ends there.

Marie T. Freeman

Let your old age be childlike,
and childhood like old age; that is, so that
neither may your wisdom be with pride,
nor your humility without wisdom.

St. Augustine

Let the word of Christ dwell in you richly in all wisdom;
teaching and admonishing one another in psalms
and hymns and spiritual songs, singing with grace
in your hearts to the Lord.

Colossians 3:16 KJV

∼ A Prayer ∼

Heavenly Father, Your Holy Word is a light unto
the world; we will study it, trust it, and share it.
In all that we do, help us be worthy witnesses
for You as we share the Good News
of Your perfect Son and Your perfect Word.
Amen

∼ More Verses to Consider ∼

Matthew 7:24
Proverbs 10:14
Psalm 107:43
Daniel 12:3

28

Beyond Perfectionism

Above all, love each other deeply,
because love covers a multitude of sins.

1 Peter 4:8 NIV

Expectations, expectations, expectations! As a dues-paying citizen of the 21st century, you know that demands can be high, and expectations even higher. The media delivers an endless stream of messages that tell you how to look, how to behave, how to eat, and how to dress. The media's expectations are impossible to meet—God's are not. God doesn't expect perfection . . . and neither should you.

The difference between perfectionism and realistic expectations is the difference between a life of frustration and a life of contentment. Only one earthly being ever lived life to perfection, and He was the Son of God. The rest of us have fallen short of God's standard and need to be accepting of our own limitations as well as the limitations of others.

If you find you or your spouse are bound up by the chains of perfectionism, it's time to ask yourself who you're trying to impress, and why. If you're trying to impress your friends, or if you're trying to imitate the appearance of some rail-thin Hollywood celebrity, it's time to reconsider your priorities. Your first responsibility is to the heavenly Father who created you and to the Son who saved you. Then, you bear a powerful responsibility to your spouse and your family. But, when it comes to meeting society's unrealistic expectations, forget it!

Remember that when you accepted Christ as your Savior, God accepted you for all eternity. Now, it's *your* turn to accept yourself *and* your loved ones. When you do, you'll feel a tremendous weight being lifted from your shoulders. After all, pleasing God is simply a matter of obeying His commandments and accepting His Son. But as for pleasing everybody else? *That's* impossible!

The happiest people in the world are not those who have no problems, but the people who have learned to live with those things that are less than perfect.

James Dobson

What makes a Christian a Christian is not perfection but forgiveness.

Max Lucado

I want you to remember what a difference there is between perfection and perfectionism.
The former is a Bible truth; the latter may or may not be a human perversion of the truth.
I fear that many, in their horror of perfectionism, reject perfection too.

Andrew Murray

Kind people do themselves a favor,
but cruel people bring trouble on themselves.

Proverbs 11:17 NCV

A Prayer

Dear Lord, You have taught us that love covers
a multitude of shortcomings. Keep us mindful
that perfection will be ours in the next world,
not in this one. Help us to be accepting of our
own imperfections, and give us the wisdom to accept—
and even to cherish—the imperfections of
those we love.
Amen

More Verses to Consider

Ephesians 4:32
James 3:17
Luke 6:37
1 Peter 3:8

29

A Shared Faith

---

*Now I plead with you, brethren, by the name of our Lord
Jesus Christ, that you all speak the same thing, and that there
be no divisions among you, but that you be perfectly joined
together in the same mind and in the same judgment.*

1 Corinthians 1:10 NKJV

Would you and your spouse like to strengthen the bonds of your marriage? Here's a wonderful place to start: by strengthening your faith in God.

Every life and every marriage is a series of successes and failures, celebrations and disappointments, joys and sorrows. Every step of the way, through every triumph and tragedy, God will stand by your side and strengthen you . . . *if* you have faith in Him. Jesus taught His disciples that if they had faith, they could move mountains. You can too.

When a suffering woman sought healing by merely touching the hem of His cloak, Jesus replied, "Daughter, be of good comfort; thy faith hath made thee whole" (Matthew 9:22 KJV). The message to believers of every generation is clear: we must live by faith today and every day.

When you and your spouse place your faith, your trust, indeed your life in the hands of Christ Jesus, you'll be amazed at the marvelous things He can do with you and through you. So strengthen your faith *and* your marriage through praise, through worship, through Bible study, and through prayer. And trust God's plans. With Him, all things are possible, and He stands ready to open a world of possibilities to you and yours . . . *if* you have faith.

It is possible to be close to people physically
and miles away from them spiritually.

Warren Wiersbe

With resolve that you are going to make
a relationship work, you can develop peace treaties
of love and tolerance and harmony to transform
a difficult situation into something beautiful.

Max Lucado

We've grown to be one soul—two parts;
our lives are so intertwined that when
some passion stirs your heart,
I feel the quake in mine.

Gloria Gaither

As I grew older, I realized that my parents' love for
one another was deeper than just the look in their eyes
each time one of them came into the room.
Their love was based on more than their physical
and emotional attraction. It was based on solid,
uncompromising commitment, first to Jesus Christ,
and second to the institution of marriage.

Gigi Graham Tchividjian

Do not be unequally yoked together . . . .

2 Corinthians 6:14 NKJV

❧ A Prayer ❧

Dear Lord, keep us mindful that You are always near
and that You can overcome any challenge.
With Your love and Your power, Father,
we can live courageously
and faithfully today and every day.
Amen

❧ More Verses to Consider ❧

2 Timothy 2:8
Psalm 133:1
1 Corinthians 12:12-31

30

God Is Love

We know how much God loves us, and we have
put our trust in him. God is love, and all who live in love
live in God, and God lives in them.

1 John 4:16 NLT

Make no mistake about it: God loves our world. He loves it so much, in fact, that He sent His only begotten Son to die for our sins. And now we, as believers, are challenged to return God's love by obeying His commandments and honoring His Son.

When you and your spouse allow Christ to reign over your lives and your marriage, you will be transformed: you will feel differently about yourselves, your marriage, your family, and your world. When you and your beloved feel God's presence and invite His Son to rule your hearts and your household, your family will be eternally blessed.

God loved this world so much that He sent His Son to save it. And now only one real question remains: what will you and yours do in response to God's love? The answer should be obvious: If you haven't already done so, accept Jesus Christ as Your Savior. He's waiting patiently for you, but *please* don't make Him wait another minute longer.

No part of our prayers creates a greater feeling of joy
than when we praise God for who He is.
He is our Master Creator, our Father,
our source of all love.

Shirley Dobson

God's love did not begin at Calvary.
Before the world was baptized with the first light,
before the first blades of tender grass peeped out,
God was love.

Billy Graham

When did God's love for you begin?
When He began to be God.
When did He begin to be God?
Never, for He has always been without beginning
and without end, and so He has always
loved you from eternity.

Francis de Sales

Though our feelings come and go,
God's love for us does not.

C. S. Lewis

We love Him because He first loved us.

1 John 4:19 NKJV

A Prayer

Lord, Your love is infinite and eternal.
Although we cannot fully understand the depths
of Your love, we can praise it, return it,
and share it always. Make our love for others
and our love for You a shining example to our family
and to all whom You place along our path,
today and forever.
Amen

More Verses to Consider

Ephesians 1:4-5
Psalm 103:17-18
Romans 5:8
Romans 8:35,38-39